In the Camps

Teens Who Survived
the Nazi Concentration Camps

North Sea

DENMARK

SWEDEN

Baltic Sea

LATVIA
• Jungernhof

LITHUANIA
Ninth Fort (Kovno)
Ponar (Vilna)

• Ravensbrück   • Treblinka
• Sachsenhausen
• Bergen-Belsen   • Warsaw   • Sobibor

NETHERLANDS   • Buchenwald   • Gross-Rosen   ▲ Łódź
• Westerbork   • Majdanek
Amsterdam   Berlin
•Vught   • Grünberg   ▲ • Theresienstadt   POLAND
BELGIUM   • Hadamar   ▲ Sosnowiec   • Belzec
Brussels   • ▲ Plaszow   ▲ Lvov
GERMANY   • Auschwitz
LUXEMBOURG   ▲ Cracow   UKRAINE

SOVIET

UNION

CZECHOSLOVAKIA

• Dachau   • Mauthausen
Vienna   Odessa
AUSTRIA   ▲ Budapest   Chisinau
SWITZERLAND   HUNGARY   ROMANIA

• Concentration Camp
▲ Major Ghetto

In the Camps

Teens Who Survived the Nazi Concentration Camps

by Toby Axelrod

THE ROSEN PUBLISHING GROUP, INC.
NEW YORK

Dedicated to the memory of my grandfather, Rabbi Jacob Axelrod, whose stories about his youth in a small Polish town helped me understand the world that was destroyed in the Holocaust. With profound thanks to historian Dr. Jud Newborn of New York's Museum of Jewish Heritage—A Living Memorial to the Holocaust, and to fellow journalist Steve Lipman of the New York Jewish Week, *who inspire me with their fine work and their friendship.*

Published in 1999 by The Rosen Publishing Group, Inc.
29 East 21st Street, New York, NY 10010

First Edition

Library of Congress Cataloging-in-Publication Data

Axelrod, Toby.
    In the camps : teens who survived the Nazi concentration camps.
  —1st ed.
        p. cm. — (Teen witnesses to the Holocaust)
  Includes bibliographical references and index.
  SUMMARY: Relates the stories of Jewish teenagers who were sent to Nazi concentration camps where they were separated from their families and survived years of exhausting labor, scarce food, and cruel guards.
  ISBN 0-8239-2844-6
  1. Jewish children in the Holocaust—Biography.   2. Jewish teenagers—Biography. [1. Holocaust, Jewish (1939–1945)—Personal narratives. 2. Jews—Biography.] I. Title. II. Series.
D804.195.A87 1999
940.53'18'083—dc21
                                                          98-32232
                                                             CIP
                                                              AC

Manufactured in the United States of America

Contents

Introduction

It is important for everyone to learn about the Holocaust, the systematic murder of 6 million Jews during World War II (1939–1945). It is a dark scar across the face of human history. As a student, you are part of the future generation that will lead and guide the family of humankind. Your proper understanding of the Holocaust is essential. You will learn its lessons. You will be able to ensure that a Holocaust will never happen again and that the world will be a safe place for each person—regardless of his or her nationality, religion, or ethnicity.

Nazi Germany added a dangerous new element to the familiar concept of "dislike of the unlike." The Nazis introduced the idea that an *ethnic group* whom someone dislikes or hates can be isolated from the rest of the population and earmarked for total destruction, *without any possibility of survival.*

The Nazis chose the Jewish people for this fatal annihilation. Their definition of a Jew was a uniquely racial one: a person with Jewish blood. To the Nazis, a person with even one Jewish grandparent was a Jew—a person to be killed.

The Germans systematically rounded up Jews in the countries that they occupied during World War II. They built death camps equipped with the most sophisticated technology available in order to kill the Jews. With the assistance of collaborators (non-Germans who willingly helped), they murdered more than 6 million Jews. Among the victims were 1.5 million children and teenagers. These Jewish children, like Jewish adults, had no options. They were murdered because they had Jewish blood, and nothing they could do could change that.

Such a thing had never happened before in recorded history, despite the fact that genocide (deliberate destruction of people of one

Background: The Nazis categorized concentration camp prisoners into different groups: Jews, political prisoners, homosexuals, etc. This chart shows the system of patches used to distinguish among categories of prisoners.

ethnic, political, or cultural group) had occurred. In the past, victims or oppressed people were usually offered an option to avoid death: they could change their religion, or be expelled to another country. But the Nazi concept of racism did not give the victim any possibility for survival, since a person cannot change his or her blood, skin color, or eye color.

A few non-Jewish people, known as the Righteous Among the Nations, saved Jews from death. They felt that they were their brothers' and sisters' keepers. But they were in the minority. The majority were collaborators or bystanders. During the Holocaust, I was a young child saved by several Righteous Poles. The majority of my family and the Jews of my town, many of whose families had lived there for 900 years, were murdered by the Nazis with the assistance of local collaborators. Photographs of those who were murdered gaze upon visitors to the Tower of Life exhibit that I designed for the United States Holocaust Memorial Museum in Washington, D.C.

We must learn the lessons of the Holocaust. We must learn to respect one another, regardless of differences in religion, ethnicity, or race, since we all belong to the family of humankind. The United States and Canada are both countries of immigrants, populated by many ethnic groups. In lands of such diversity, dislike of the unlike— the Nazi idea of using racial classification as a reason to destroy other humans—is dangerous to all of us. If we allow intolerance toward one group of people today, any of us could be part of a group selected for destruction tomorrow. Understanding and respecting one another regardless of religion, race, or ethnicity is essential for coexistence and survival.

In this book individuals who were teenagers during the Holocaust share their experiences of life before and during the war and of the days of liberation. Their messages about their families, friends, love, suffering, survival, liberation, and rebuilding of new lives are deeply inspiring. They are important because these survivors are among the last eyewitnesses, the last links to what happened during the Holocaust.

I hope that their stories will encourage you to build a better, safer future "with liberty and justice for all."

Yaffa Eliach, Ph.D.
Professor of History and Literature
Department of Judaic Studies, Brooklyn College

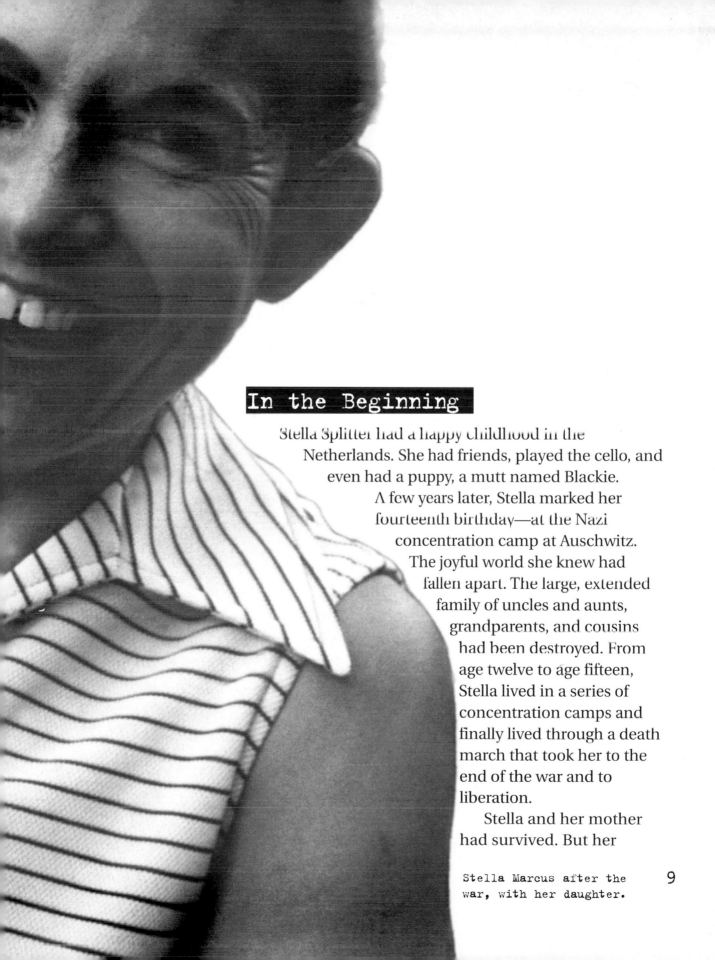

In the Beginning

Stella Splitter had a happy childhood in the Netherlands. She had friends, played the cello, and even had a puppy, a mutt named Blackie.

A few years later, Stella marked her fourteenth birthday—at the Nazi concentration camp at Auschwitz. The joyful world she knew had fallen apart. The large, extended family of uncles and aunts, grandparents, and cousins had been destroyed. From age twelve to age fifteen, Stella lived in a series of concentration camps and finally lived through a death march that took her to the end of the war and to liberation.

Stella and her mother had survived. But her

Stella Marcus after the war, with her daughter.

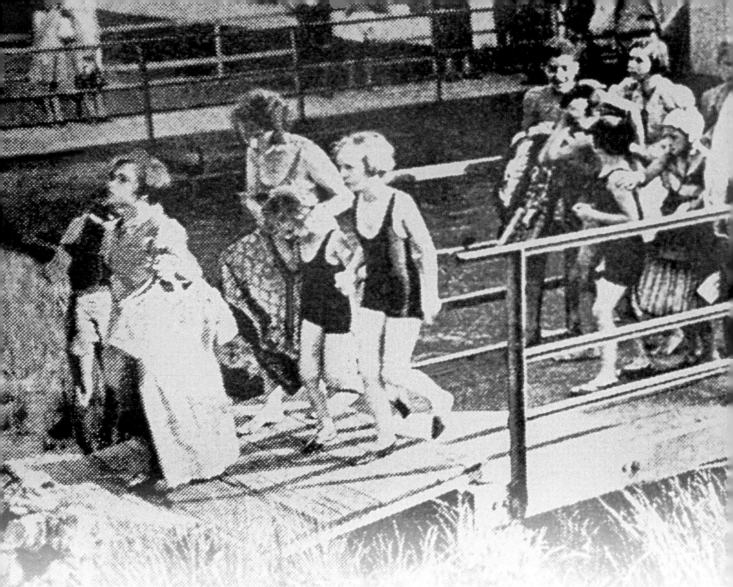

father was dead, along with most of the rest of the family. Life began again; Stella moved to the United States, where she met her future husband, Hank Marcus, who had survived the war in hiding in Amsterdam, the Netherlands. The Marcuses had a child, and they are very proud of her. There is much happiness in their lives. But Stella will always remember her early teen years, when almost everything precious was destroyed.

Teens Under the Nazis

Imagine not being able to go to the movies with a friend, because you are Jewish; or taking your date to the only place where Jews are allowed to meet: the cemetery; or being kicked out of your school—

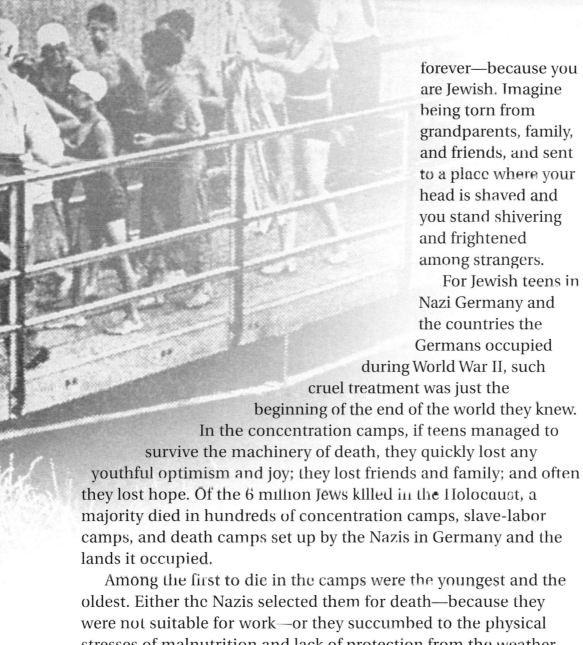

forever—because you are Jewish. Imagine being torn from grandparents, family, and friends, and sent to a place where your head is shaved and you stand shivering and frightened among strangers.

For Jewish teens in Nazi Germany and the countries the Germans occupied during World War II, such cruel treatment was just the beginning of the end of the world they knew. In the concentration camps, if teens managed to survive the machinery of death, they quickly lost any youthful optimism and joy; they lost friends and family; and often they lost hope. Of the 6 million Jews killed in the Holocaust, a majority died in hundreds of concentration camps, slave-labor camps, and death camps set up by the Nazis in Germany and the lands it occupied.

Among the first to die in the camps were the youngest and the oldest. Either the Nazis selected them for death—because they were not suitable for work—or they succumbed to the physical stresses of malnutrition and lack of protection from the weather and disease. By contrast, those who survived the horrors of the concentration camps were likely to be those who entered the camps able to work. Of those, many were teenagers.

Following are the stories of several people who, like Stella, were teenagers under the dark cloud of Nazism. Theirs are stories of courage, fear, anguish, and in the end, hope.

Jewish children being ejected from a public swimming pool in Bad Herweck, Mannheim, Germany, 1938.

chapter two

Nazi Concentration Camps

The first Nazi concentration camps were built in Germany as detention centers for political prisoners, people who opposed the Nazis. Later, as Hitler's determination to kill the Jews was translated into national policy, many more such camps were built, both in Germany and in Nazi-occupied lands. They ranged from slave-labor camps, where people often were worked to death, to death camps such as Auschwitz-Birkenau in Poland, where thousands of people were killed each day within minutes or hours of their arrival.

At Auschwitz-Birkenau, mass killing took place in gas chambers, which were disguised as showers. Prisoners were forced to remove the victims' bodies and bring them to a crematorium, where the remains would be burned. Later, the prisoners who had been forced to help in this work would be killed themselves. By the time Auschwitz was liberated by the Soviet army in January 1945, about 2 million people had been murdered there by the Nazis.

Who Were the Nazis?

In 1932, Germany was struggling. It had lost World War I. Many Germans resented the fact that the Allies, including the United

States, had
forced them
to pay millions
of dollars in
reparations to the
nations Germany had
attacked. Many Germans,
including Jews, thought their
country had been treated
unfairly.

Hitler was an answer to their
complaints. He said he would create jobs
and strengthen his country. He claimed
Germans were superior and could again be a
great and powerful people.

Hitler became chancellor of Germany in 1933.
His political party, the National Socialists, or Nazis,
had won one-third of the votes in the election of
November 1932. It still wasn't a majority. But none of the
other parties had enough votes to beat the Nazis.

Hitler's Brand of Antisemitism

Hitler publicly blamed Germany's problems on a tiny percent of its
population, the Jews. It was known that Hitler was antisemitic, because
he had expressed this in his book, *Mein Kampf.*

In *Mein Kampf,* Hitler wrote that the sole purpose of the govern-

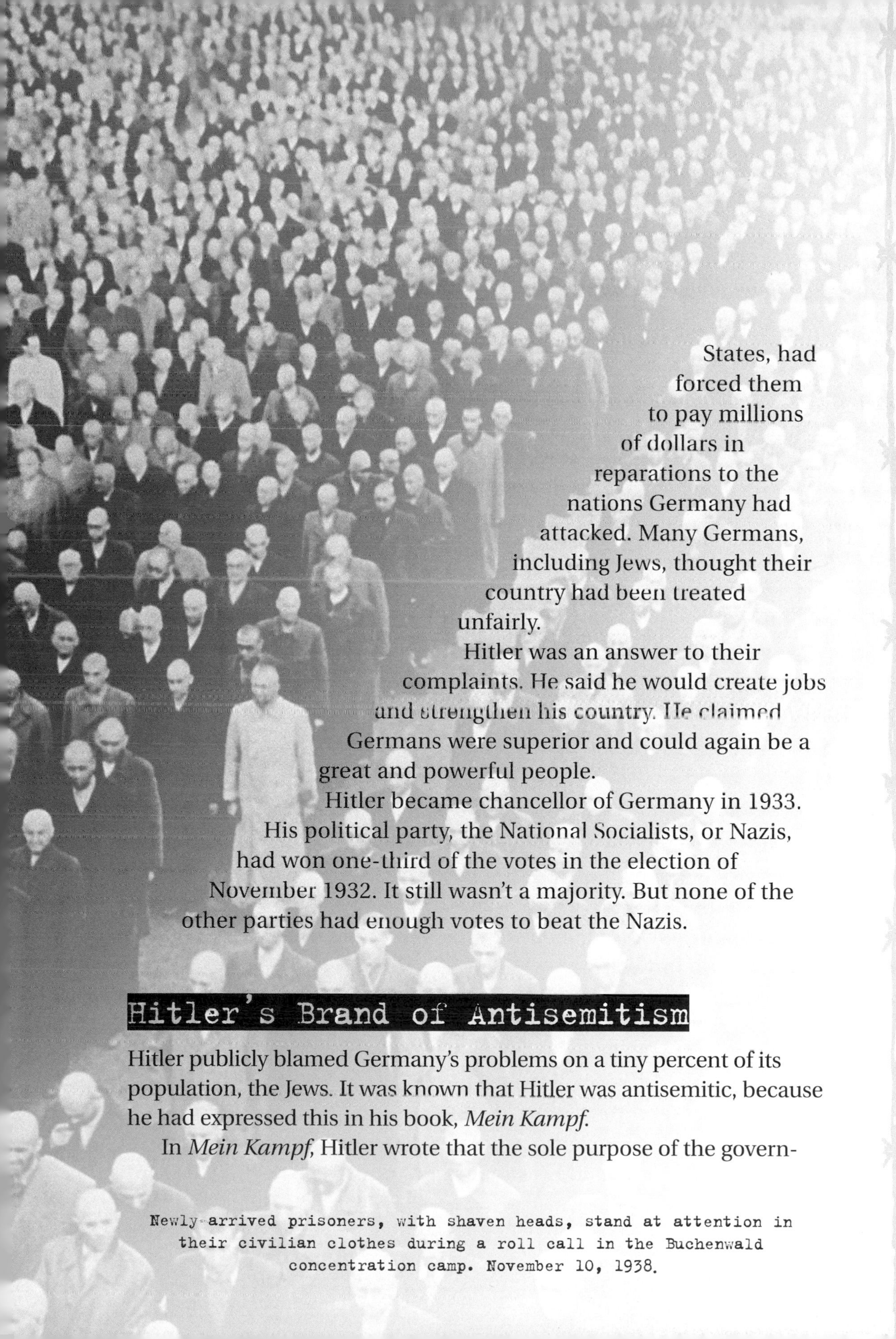

Newly arrived prisoners, with shaven heads, stand at attention in
their civilian clothes during a roll call in the Buchenwald
concentration camp. November 10, 1938.

In the 1930s, many of Germany's Jews were secular, meaning they were not very religious, and lived like other German citizens, in villages and cities. As children they went to school and played with friends, and later they attended college and got jobs. Most of them had been born in Germany. They identified themselves as Germans and were proud of their national heritage, with its great composers, poets, and philosophers. At that time, Jews made up less than one percent of the population of Germany.

ment was to guard the "racial purity" of the German people, who were "Aryans." He said that Aryans were the "master race," which was supposed to rule the world. The solution to Germany's problems, Hitler claimed, involved understanding "the racial problem and hence . . . the Jewish problem."

Hitler falsely claimed that Jews were a distinct race, one whose goal it was to control the world. He believed that Jews were lying when they called Judaism a religion. He believed that Jewish genes were at the root of Germany's problems.

Just as racist attitudes exist today among some Americans, in the early 1930s, antisemitic views were not uncommon in Germany. In the beginning, Hitler and his supporters sounded just a little louder than a lot of other people.

An Explosion of Hatred

Once in power, Hitler began to change Germany's government. It had been democratic; now, Hitler gave himself many extra powers as ruler, claiming that Germany was in a state of emergency. His title was *Führer*—leader. He even had power over the German president, Paul von Hindenburg. Soon after becoming chancellor in January 1933, Hitler convinced Hindenburg to give the police the authority to prohibit public gatherings and to censor publications. Now Hitler could control the police and the press.

When Hindenburg died in August 1934, Hitler became president and chancellor. He was on his way to total control of the country.

The Nazis began to enact laws that curtailed the rights of Jewish citizens. Little by little, Jews were forced to give up their jobs, property, and businesses. Jewish students were taken out of public schools and forced into special Jewish schools.

Travel was restricted, and Jewish homes were marked with a Star of David. These changes took place gradually but steadily. Vandalism of Jewish-owned shops became common, and police often looked the other way. Prejudice against Jews became institutionalized, a policy of the state that its police and citizens were expected to carry out.

The Nuremberg Laws of 1935 took persecution a step farther, giving an official, pseudoscientific definition of the so-called "Jewish race." Anyone with at least one Jewish grandparent was considered to be Jewish and had to submit to the laws restricting Jews.

Three years later, on the night of November 9, 1938, Nazi thugs carried out a government-sponsored attack on Jews and Jewish property. Hundreds of German and Austrian synagogues were left in ruins, and Jewish-owned businesses were looted and destroyed. Some 100 Jews were murdered, and 30,000 Jewish men were imprisoned in German concentration camps on that day. This night of terror came to be called Kristallnacht, or the night of broken glass.

By mid-1939, about 300,000 Jews had managed to emigrate from Germany. Tragically, many fled to parts of Europe that soon came under German occupation. Many would later become victims of the Holocaust.

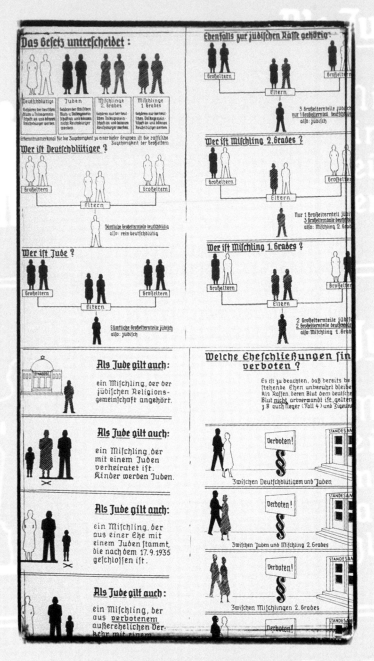

A chart showing the ways the Nazis defined who was a Jew. Germans who had Jewish grandparents, for example, were subject to some of the same restrictions as Jews themselves, as were non-Jews married to Jews.

The Nazis developed their concentration camps and death camps gradually, starting in 1933. One of Hitler's first goals was to silence his enemies before they had a chance to speak. Many Germans who were seen as threats to the Nazi government would be sent to the German detention centers in Dachau, Buchenwald, and Sachsenhausen, for hard labor and other punishment. By the summer of 1933, there were ten Nazi prison camps with more than 25,000 prisoners.

In the beginning, such prisoners might have had hopes of coming home. Later, these camps turned into slave-labor camps where prisoners were forced to work to help Germany win the war. On a starvation diet, with little clothing, and performing heavy labor, most prisoners became deathly ill, emaciated, and weak. Those unable to work usually would be removed and killed or left to die. Then more prisoners would arrive to take their places.

War Begins

On September 1, 1939, Germany invaded Poland. This was part of a larger military plan to seize control of much of Europe in order to establish *Lebensraum*, or living space, for Germans. Hitler ordered that Jews, Poles, and other non-Germans be removed from the "old and new Reich area" to make room for so-called pure Germans.

The German army invaded country after country. Jews in the newly occupied lands were removed from their homes, under threat or by force, and placed in heavily guarded ghettos across occupied Europe.

Before being forced to leave their homes, Jews had to give up most of their belongings. Many Jews had lived simply, in rural villages. Others had valuable possessions, such as jewelry and paintings. The Germans put stolen valuables in banks or hid them elsewhere for the use of the Reich. They sold the rest—including beds and tablecloths—for profit.

Confined in overcrowded ghettos, the Jews lived in impoverished conditions, with insufficient food, heat, medicine, and clothing. Many died as a result of disease, starvation, and lack of protection from the elements. Bringing the Jews together in ghettos made it easier for the Nazis to deport them in large groups to concentration camps later.

Two years later, following Germany's invasion of the Soviet Union in 1941, the Nazis adopted a brutal policy toward Jews living in lands invaded by the Nazis: after the German army occupied a new territory, special mobile killing squads known as *Einsatzgruppen* went into action. They rounded up Jews and other "enemies" of the Nazis—often with the assistance of local collaborators—and executed them.

The Nazis devised a system to murder all of European Jewry through mass executions. In 1941, several concentration camps were built for the specific purpose of killing. The first to be completed was Chelmno, in Poland.

By the summer of 1942, camps for gassing had also been built in Belzec, Majdanek, and Treblinka, all in Poland. The Nazis began to send the Jews from the ghettos to the death camps.

Within Germany, Hitler was carrying out his belief that non-Germans and others would pollute the "Aryan" nation. Those he considered "inferior" were slated for death: Jews; people politically opposed to the Nazis; Roma and Sinti (Gypsies); people who might be homosexual; and people who were physically handicapped or considered mentally ill. Handicapped people were a "drain" on the economy, Hitler argued, because they needed to be supported. So they were the first group to be killed in large numbers, in special centers set up in Germany. To make it sound better, the Nazis called their dirty work euthanasia, or mercy killing. Tens of thousands of physically and mentally disabled Germans were killed under this program.

Washing and shaving newly arrived prisoners in the Buchenwald
concentration camp, 1940.

When they arrived at the death camps, Jews faced a *Selektion*,
or Nazi selection of prisoners. Some 10 percent might be spared
immediate death and be sent to work. Those marked for death—
usually, the unfit, the very young, the elderly, and mothers with
children—would be sent to gas chambers. Sometimes, the Nazis
tried to disguise what was happening by telling the new arrivals
they were about to have showers. At other times, new arrivals
would be whipped or beaten on their way to their death.

Those who survived the initial selection usually underwent a
humiliating process: Their heads were shaved in order to remove
or prevent lice; they had to discard their clothes and belongings and
were issued prison uniforms and wooden shoes, or clogs; and at
Auschwitz, they would receive an identification tattoo. Sometimes
they would receive a cup or bowl, without which they could not
receive nourishment. A metal soup bowl could mean the difference
between life and death.

Then began months, even years of labor, some of it excruciatingly
exhausting. Food and water were scarce. Camp guards were often

Opposite page: View of the Hadamar Institute, one of six hospitals and
nursing facilities in which the Nazi euthanasia program was carried
out. Hadamar, Germany, 1941.

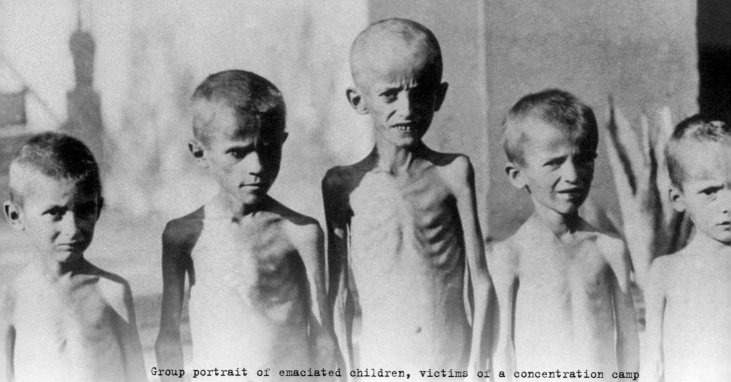

Group portrait of emaciated children, victims of a concentration camp for children in Yugoslavia. 1942-1944.

cruel. Regular selections by the Nazi guards led to the removal of the weak or sick. Those "selected" would never be seen again. While struggling to survive against these odds, most inmates had to contend with the fact that their families and friends were probably dead. Sometimes the pain was too great, and prisoners took their own lives.

Not the Germans Alone

Meanwhile, Hitler's paranoid claim that Jews wanted to control the world was actually a fitting description of his own goals.

By the end of the war, Germany had occupied most of Europe and parts of Scandinavia and the former Soviet Union. With the exception of Denmark, occupied countries assisted in the German policy against Jews.

Italy, which was Germany's ally, also introduced restrictions against Jews. In addition, several countries allied themselves to Germany and its wartime allies: Bulgaria, Hungary, Romania, and parts of Yugoslavia.

Ultimately, of some 9 million Jews who lived in those later-occupied areas before the war, some 6 million were killed by the Nazis in mass executions or in the death camps.

chapter three

Without God, It Is Even More Cruel

"I was not average," says Professor David Weiss Halivni, recalling his youth in Romania. He is sitting in his apartment on New York City's west side. "Learning was the dominating force in my life."

When the Nazis came to the Carpathian Mountains in 1944, David was sixteen years old and already a renowned rabbinical student. He lived in Sighet, Romania, with his grandfather Rabbi Shaye Weiss, his aunt, his sister, and his mother. His parents were separated.

David was born in 1928. "If life had been undisturbed, I would be a rabbi in a small village. I probably would have been married at eighteen, and I would have married a rabbi's daughter," says David.

But in 1938 Hungary invaded part of Romania; four years later, Germany invaded Romania. When the Nazis forced the Jews of Sighet into a ghetto, David focused on religious studies, including study of the Jewish holy works, the Torah and the Talmud, and not on the events of the world around him.

One month later, on May 15, 1944, David, his grandfather, his

mother, his aunt, and his sister were sent to Auschwitz.
Soon after we arrived in Auschwitz, I lost sight of my mother, my sister, and my aunt. I did not see them again.

David stayed beside his grandfather.

Growing Up

As a boy, David enjoyed playing ball and a game that involved throwing nuts against a wall. But he was known as a prodigy in Jewish learning, and one day a neighbor remarked, "A child who knows Talmud shouldn't be playing nuts." David was embarrassed, and he stopped playing. In fact,his knowledge of Jewish books was remarkable, and rabbis enjoyed listening to this boy explain complicated passages.

I took shelter in the protective coat of learning. Any learning which connects you with the past separates you from anything else.

In Sighet, David did not attend the public school. He went to a religious school instead. But he always wanted to learn nonreligious subjects as well. He spent a lot of time with his eighty-year-old grandfather, who was also a best friend.

Some people went to Germany to study. It would have caused such heartbreak for the family if I did that. I wasn't the type to leave home—especially because I learned so much from my grandfather. I could not do anything that would have broken his heart.

At Auschwitz, Dr. Josef Mengele, the camp physician responsible for sending millions to their deaths, separated David from his grandfather. He never saw his grandfather again. Out of his grandfather's children, grandchildren, and great-grandchildren— sixty-four in all—only five would survive the war.

The Stonecutters and the Bletl

About a week after arriving at Auschwitz, David was transferred to a camp in Germany called Gross-Rosen. He was forced to work on a team that cut stones for building roads.

Between hard labor, some men would study Jewish texts together, as they used to do at home. Because they weren't allowed to have any books, they had to do it from memory. David, who knew the books by heart, became their leader.

Then a small miracle occurred. One day, David spotted a sentry eating a sandwich wrapped in a *bletl*, a page from a Jewish religious text.

Seeing the bletl, *I fell at his feet with tears in my eyes and begged, "Please give it to me." He put his hand on his revolver—but after a few moments, he gave the* bletl *to me.*

That one page—Paragraph 434 of the laws of Passover—became the focus of these learned men, and one of them, a Mr. Finkelstein, was entrusted to keep it.

And Mr. Finkelstein risked his life to keep it. We used to hold it. It was covered with grease spots. It was dangerous to be caught with it. We didn't study it all the time—but the bletl *was always there.*

In February 1945, David and other inmates were forced on a two-month death march to Ebensee, part of the complex of camps around Mauthausen, Austria. The Nazis were fleeing from the advancing Russian army, who were approaching Gross-Rosen, and were trying to remove all evidence of the concentration camps, including people. Less

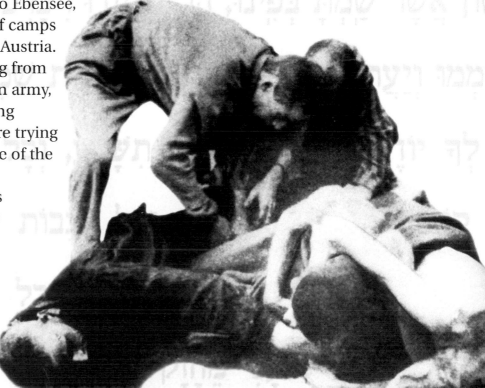

Right: Hungry prisoners in Mauthausen concentration camp fight for a slice of bread, April 1945.

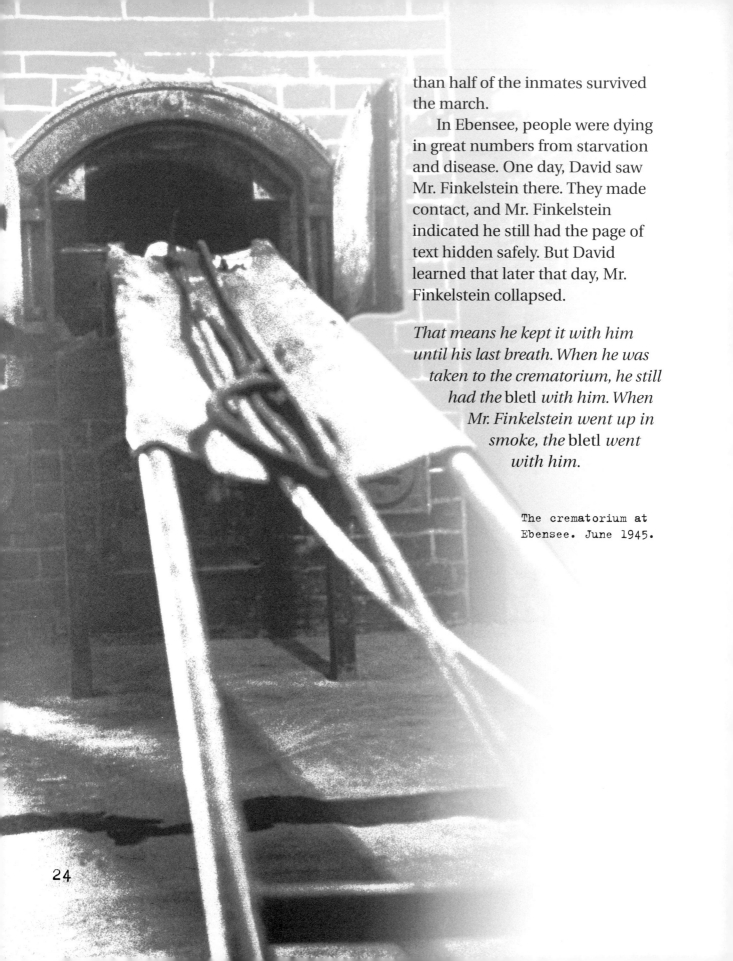

than half of the inmates survived the march.

In Ebensee, people were dying in great numbers from starvation and disease. One day, David saw Mr. Finkelstein there. They made contact, and Mr. Finkelstein indicated he still had the page of text hidden safely. But David learned that later that day, Mr. Finkelstein collapsed.

That means he kept it with him until his last breath. When he was taken to the crematorium, he still had the bletl *with him. When Mr. Finkelstein went up in smoke, the* bletl *went with him.*

The crematorium at Ebensee. June 1945.

24

Doubts and Faith

Although his faith was tested, David never lost his belief in God.

I had philosophical questions and doubts: Since there were so many cruelties, God cannot exist. He would not have permitted it.
    But without God, it is even more cruel.
    God gave man the power, and God gave man his free will.

Liberation and Beyond

On May 6, 1945, American troops liberated Mauthausen and Ebensee.

I was too tired to get up when they told me, "Americans are outside." I was weak, and I had a bed all to myself. The Americans found me.

When he had recovered his strength, David returned to Sighet, but "I was there less than ten days.". David lived in Germany for two years. He arrived in the United States in 1947.

Background: Liberated survivors eagerly pull down the Nazi eagle over the entrance to the Mauthausen concentration camp. May 6, 1945.

Tzipora Hager Halivni grew up in Viseul de Sus, Romania, where her father was a rabbi.

Tzipora's parents were visiting Hungary in March 1944 when the Germans invaded. Her mother escaped and returned to Romania. Her father was captured trying to escape and died a prisoner on a Nazi freight train.

In May 1944, Germany invaded Romania. Tzipora was deported to Auschwitz with her grandmother, her brother Naftali, who was thirteen, and her youngest brother, Menachem, who was two-and-a-half. In the selection line, Tzipora was separated from the rest of her family.

Tzipora says that at Auschwitz she had become a different person. "From the minute you put your foot down in the encirclement, you are forlorn. Literally, I felt that this was not me."

She speaks of the vehemence of hunger, which led her to do something she normally would not do. She picked up a piece of bread that some unknown person had left on the ground. She hesitated, but someone told her, "Hush, take it." It lasted two days.

Everyone had a different way of dealing with the ever-present companion, hunger, says Tzipora. "Day after day, you see your body dropping," she remembers. "But there was a stomach. There was no room for sleep. Was there room for hope? There was room for dreaming.

"Occasionally, I would allow myself to dream: 'I will go out and eat, and my hair will grow in, and my face will look good, and my dress will be beautiful, and I will meet my mother.' Is there a better dream than that?"

Tzipora was in Auschwitz for three months and then sent to a slave-labor camp in Fallersleben, Germany, where she worked in a weapons factory.

One part of the weapon was a large metal plate the size of an oversized dinner plate. In the center of it was a hole (the size of my wrist) that had metal threads inside it. A small plate with matching metal threads was screwed into it.

My job was to let this device down into the water with the help of a mechanical arm. If air bubbles appeared between the two plates, the device was defective; the weapon would not explode in the field. I was supposed to check each device and remove the defective ones.

When I arrived at Fallersleben, a Polish Kapo who did not speak German trained me to do my job, watching me carefully for three days to make certain I did it right. At first I did, and removed the defective devices.

But after a few weeks I learned to fault the gadget. Most of the time I let the plate down and up so fast that I could not see—bubbles? no bubbles?—in the water. I sabotaged the work. I had to remove some plates, of course, or the Kapos would have become suspicious. Some that I removed really were defective; others were not. Some that were defective were allowed to go through.

Three months later, our entire group went to work elsewhere, which saved me from the Germans having noticed the damage I had done.

Tzipora was liberated from the labor camp on her sixteenth birthday, May 10, 1945. Her mother and brother Naftali also survived. They emigrated to the United States. There Tzipora met and married David Weiss Halivni.

chapter four

Reservoirs of Strength

"Everybody suffered in the Nazi concentration camps," recalls Gerda Weissmann Klein. "I was not unique." Gerda was born in Bielsko, Poland, in 1924. She and her older brother, Arthur, and their parents, Julius and Helene, had a comfortable life in the picturesque mountain town where tourists would come for vacation. Gerda's father was a partner in a fur-producing factory. Her mother was a homemaker.

Gerda's happy teenage years came to an end on September 3, 1939, when the Nazis marched into her town. Bielsko "had always been so safe and secure," Gerda wrote in her autobiography, *All But My Life*, which was first published in 1957 and was made into an Academy Award-winning HBO documentary in 1995.

The last happy memory I took with me was my fifteenth birthday. Many friends came, and we had an afternoon party in our garden house, with cake and ice cream and all. A few months later, the horror was unleashed.

Neighbors started shouting, "Heil Hitler!" and welcoming the German troops. This began the almost total destruction of everything I knew, and every step was fraught with danger. It was extremely risky for men to go outside because the Nazis might stop them, and they would never be seen again. Due to a recent illness, my father was completely immobilized. His role had always been a dominant one in the house. Mother had always stayed in the background. Now they were thrust into a reversal of roles.

We realized that some of my friends were Nazis when they stopped talking to me. These former friends would not come to the house anymore. My Jewish friends were very supportive.

Most of them did not survive.

By the time the war was over, Gerda had come close to death. She went through several concentration camps. She worked as a slave laborer, and hoped and prayed that she would be reunited with her family in spite of everything. But she was the only survivor in her immediate family.

Faced with Nazi Horror

When I was fifteen my brother was deported to the easternmost part of Poland. Three years later, my parents and I suffered a similar fate. We were separated and sent to different destinations; in my parents' case, Auschwitz. But at the time we were told that we were all being taken to labor camps.

Gerda was sent to a *Durchgangslager,* or transit camp (a stopping point on the way to a concentration camp or death camp), at Sosnowiec, Poland, in the summer of 1942. There, people were selected to do slave labor for the German war industry. Gerda first encountered signs of starvation and disease, things that later would become a normal part of her landscape, in Sosnowiec.

On the very first day there, I saw a girl who might have been my age. Her body was pitifully emaciated, her neck overly long. I was dismayed at the sight of her and offered her my bowl of soup. Before eating it, the girl said, "God bless you. May you never know what hunger is."

This encounter left a deep impression on Gerda.

Even today it is difficult to talk about it. It was a confrontation with what was probably in store for me too. The idea that Germany planned to kill us all hovered in the background all the time. I was still longing for my parents. The probability that they were gone was always there. But it was never accepted.

A Dividing Line

Gerda was assigned to work in the women's labor camp at Bolkenhain, Germany. There she formed an even closer bond with a childhood friend, Ilse, and each of the two girls became a support system for the other. At Bolkenhain the prisoners worked at looms in a weaving mill for long hours, making cloth for Germany.

Some weeks after our arrival, I heard my name shouted out at mail call for the first time. With great excitement I tore the envelope open before realizing it was a letter I had sent to my father. On the envelope was written: "Return to sender, moved without forwarding address." I now knew that something dreadful had happened to my father. I cried for a long time and could not accept that fact.

The most difficult thing about Bolkenhain was that it represented the dividing line between relative freedom—being with my parents— and being alone. My friendships in the camps made the difference and formed an invaluable support system.

Surviving Märzdorf

In August 1943, Gerda and Ilse were moved to the labor camp at Märzdorf, where Gerda was assigned the task of bricklaying and cleaning machinery. One day when Gerda was working, a supervisor made advances at her, which she refused. He angrily promised her,

Hungarian Jewish women who have been selected for work march toward
the camp, after disinfection and head shaving. Auschwitz, May 1944.

"You'll be sorry!" Sure enough, the next day Gerda was assigned the
worst job at Märzdorf: the flax detail.

*I went to the train station with some of the other girls. Heavy bundles
of flax were being unloaded, which meant they would be thrown
down from freight cars into our arms. We had to pass them down a
line until the bundles reached a barn, where they were stacked. Soon
our arms were bloody, swollen, and infected, whipped by the prickly
fibers. That evening—exhausted after a day on the flax detail—I was
handed a shovel and forced to unload coal from a freight car.*
After several days of working day and night, Gerda felt she could
stand it no longer. She considered jumping in front of a moving
train. Gerda told her friend Ilse of her despair.

Ilse seized an unexpected opportunity to rescue Gerda from this cruel punishment. The factory director from Bolkenhain appeared at Märzdorf to select workers for a weaving mill in Landeshut. He called out Ilse's number, and Ilse, thinking quickly, urged Gerda forward, letting Gerda take her place. Then, at the last moment, Ilse convinced the director to take her as well.

Gerda and Ilse worked in Landeshut for ten months, making silk for German parachutes.

Persevering

In May 1944, Gerda and Ilse were transferred to Grünberg, the site of another textile factory. There clothing taken from prisoners at Auschwitz and other camps was shredded and recycled, made into cloth for the Germans to use. The 1,000 girls there were allowed to shower every two weeks.

Waiting in line for such a shower, I once saw a supervisor make a fist and beat a girl's face until it was bloody because she had been talking. Then he walked away swiftly without wiping his hands.

Gerda was assigned to the spinning machines. The work was grueling.

The workers in the spinning section were x-rayed every two months, a test everyone feared, because those who were found to have tuberculosis were sent to Auschwitz. Each time, my luck held, and I passed inspection.

Liberation

In January 1945, the prisoners at Grünberg and several thousand others were forced on a death march of almost four months. Out of some 2,000 girls in Gerda's column, only 120 survived. Sadly, Ilse did not. *We were liberated by American soldiers in May 1945 in the*

Dr. Daniel Weiskopf taking an X-ray of a patient in the Lodz ghetto hospital. Though the patient is smiling for the camera, these examinations were frightening for ghetto inmates, who could be deported if they were in poor health.

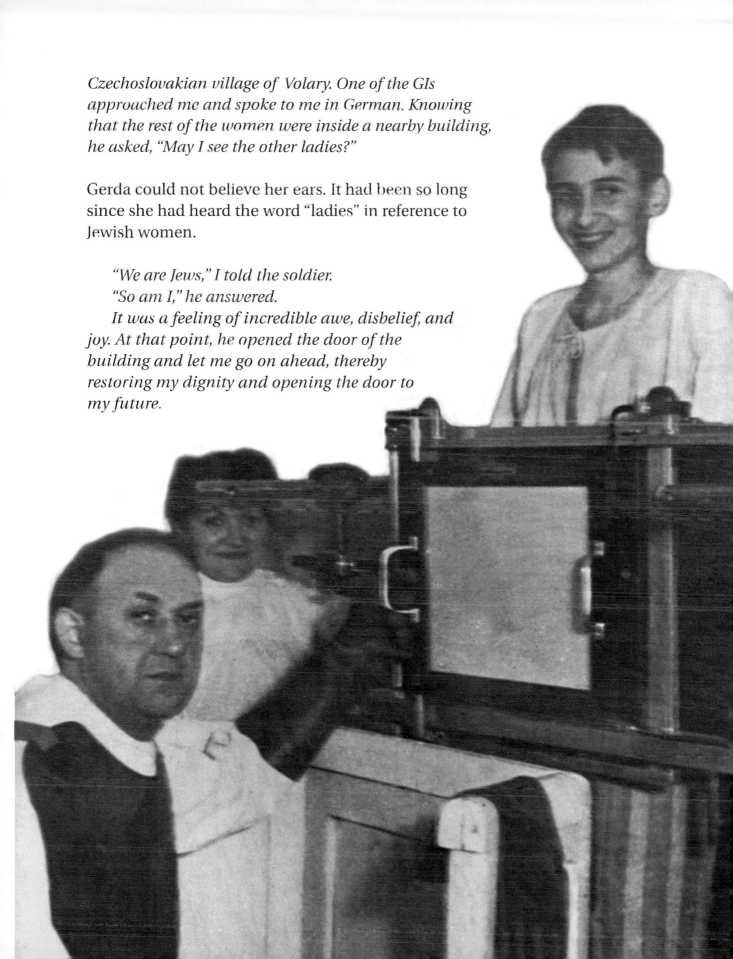

Czechoslovakian village of Volary. One of the GIs approached me and spoke to me in German. Knowing that the rest of the women were inside a nearby building, he asked, "May I see the other ladies?"

Gerda could not believe her ears. It had been so long since she had heard the word "ladies" in reference to Jewish women.

"We are Jews," I told the soldier.
"So am I," he answered.
It was a feeling of incredible awe, disbelief, and joy. At that point, he opened the door of the building and let me go on ahead, thereby restoring my dignity and opening the door to my future.

chapter five

Sometimes Miracles Happened

"I don't feel sorry for myself," Werner Reich says. Werner was fifteen when he entered the concentration camp of Theresienstadt in the former Czechoslovakia. By the end of the war two years later, he had been imprisoned in Auschwitz and Birkenau, had performed slave labor in the Mauthausen concentration camp, and had been forced to walk for days on a death march.

"My attitude and my approach to the camp was completely different from those who were thirty or forty years old in the camp," says Werner, who today talks to teens about his experiences.

As a teenager I had an invincible attitude. "Nothing can happen to me." I did not have enough worldly experience to deal with the inhumanity of man to man. Older people, who were educated and sometimes had deep religious feelings, had a completely different attitude. They couldn't take the inhumanity, and many of them committed suicide. It was very normal for people to throw themselves against the electric wire.

The bodies of two Dutch Jews who committed suicide by touching the electric barbed-wire fence in Mauthausen, Austria, 1942.

In Auschwitz, "one day, I went through selections by Dr. Josef Mengele," the doctor of the concentration camp. Many inmates called him the Angel of Death because he decided who would be sent to the gas chambers of Birkenau.

"Out of 5,000 people in that selection, ninety-eight were spared the gas chamber at that time," says Werner. "I was one of them. Sometimes miracles happened."

Before the War

Werner was born in Germany in 1927. When Hitler came to power in 1933, Werner's father, Wilhelm, lost his job an engineer with a large company called Borsig Hall. His mother, Elly, was a decorated veteran of World War I, who as a nurse had saved the lives of German soldiers. She had been awarded the military honor of an Iron Cross, with a citation that said: "The gratitude of the Fatherland will be with you forever."

Werner's father had seen a Jewish associate beaten for refusing to resign from the same company. "My father felt, 'Why should I lose my job and be beaten up?'" Werner, his older sister, Renate, and their parents left for Yugoslavia in 1933.

Seeking Safety

Werner remembers a happy childhood in Yugoslavia, before the war began. He went to Jewish summer camps, played soccer with friends, studied French. He had a stamp collection. "Sometimes on the weekend we went to a local river and did a little bit of fishing."

In 1940, his father died of kidney disease. Then in 1941, war came to Yugoslavia. Werner's mother decided to try to get American visas for her children. Her father had a dual German-American citizenship. "But the Americans would not let us go on her visa," Werner recalls. "Mother had to be on American soil before they would let the rest of us go."

She still believed nothing would happen to the family because of

Hungarian Jews in the selection line at Auschwitz. Most in the group were killed in the gas chambers only minutes after this photograph was taken. Auschwitz, Poland, spring 1944

37

her
military honors.
"But her German
medals didn't help one
iota. My mother was
arrested in 1943 and
taken to the camps."
Werner and his sister were both in Yugoslavia when the war started.
Separately, they went into hiding. "I was constantly on the run, and
constantly listening to the news, which I couldn't understand, like
hour-long speeches by Hitler," Werner recalls.

Werner was discovered by the Gestapo, the German secret police,
in 1943, when he was fifteen. He was arrested and questioned.
Eventually, he was taken to the Theresienstadt concentration camp.

In Theresienstadt, Werner had odd jobs, working in a print shop,
gardening, making baskets and brooms. He was there for less than a
year. Theresienstadt was for many a transit camp. From there, most
inmates were transported to Auschwitz-Birkenau, where they were
gassed. In 1944, Werner was sent there.

In Birkenau, the death camp connected to Auschwitz, Werner was
not selected to be gassed immediately. He was slated for work. That
included digging and carrying stones. "Later, I was transferred to
Auschwitz, where it was my job to take care of horses that belonged
to Germans, brushing and feeding them." He felt very lucky, because
the stable was warm. And he was able to eat some of the horse's
food: dried sugar beets.

*One of the worst things I saw was when a couple of prisoners tried to
escape, and they caught them. We had to stand in the yard of our
barrack while a couple of German soldiers took long poles with hooks
on either end, used for carrying barrels of food. We had to watch as
they beat them to a pulp.*

A squadron of Stuka dive bombers in action during the German invasion
of Yugoslavia. April 6, 1941.

A gas chamber at Majdanek concentration camp in Poland. The peephole
in the door allowed Nazi guards outside to watch people being killed.

In January of 1945, just before the Soviet troops liberated Auschwitz, the Nazis took the remaining inmates on a forced march through the snow to the concentration camp Mauthausen.

It was winter, and they gave us about a third of a loaf of bread before we left. After a few hours the bread froze, and there was no other food.

When the guards stopped and took a brief rest, the inmates often sat down. Many people were sitting down and they couldn't get up any more, they were too tired. We kept marching on, and they kept begging that we should help them. But we couldn't.

The Germans came and shot them.

It was utter helplessness: I couldn't help to carry or pull that person. At times I felt guilty, and at other times I felt that there was absolutely nothing I could have done. I could have prolonged that person's life by an hour or two and then died myself. It was winter, and it was very cold. There was no food. It was one of those situations when you can't do anything. It was truly hopeless.

After three days of marching, the Germans put us in open railroad cars, the type that are usually used for carrying coal. Many people died from exposure to the cold weather and the wind. Out of the thousands who left Auschwitz, only a few hundred were still alive by time we arrived in Mauthausen. My toes were frozen. A prisoner who was a doctor cut them off with a razor blade because gangrene had set in. He saved my life.

A view of the Auschwitz II camp showing the barracks of
the camp on January 29, 1945, just days after liberation.

*When we arrived, the situation in Mauthausen was very bad. The
Germans were surrounded by the Allied forces. During the last weeks of
the war, the Germans ran out of food, and we were given one
tablespoon of moldy bread a day, sometimes twice a day. People were
dying left and right. There were huge piles of bodies in the end of the
barracks.*

When one man died and the body remained in its bed, Werner took
the man's bread ration. "He stayed there for about three days," and
each day a piece of bread was "given" to the dead man. "It was a
question of survival," says Werner. "It is amazing what you will do, at
the end of the line."

The war was over. Werner returned to Yugoslavia and then went
to England, where his mother's brother lived. Werner found out that
his mother had been killed in a concentration camp.

In England, Werner met Eva, also a survivor. In 1955, they
married and moved to the United States.

chapter six

"We lived in the Netherlands and had a very good life," says Stella Marcus, smiling as she remembers her childhood in the Dutch fishing village of Scheveningen. She was born in 1930. Her family name was Splitter. It was a well-known name, because Stella's father and his four brothers had a successful fur business, with stores in the Hague and Amsterdam in the Netherlands and in Antwerp and Brussels in Belgium. "They made fur coats to order," says Stella. "When you wore a Splitter fur, everyone knew you had a very good fur coat."

Stella was an only child. A lot of her time was spent with grandparents and cousins, especially on weekends and holidays. Stella also had many good friends.

Although life was good, Stella's mother became increasingly worried about developments in nearby Germany and the Nazi occupation of part of Czechoslovakia.

As things started to get bad for Jews in Germany, my mother wanted to leave in the worst way. But my father said, "How can I leave here? We have a business. I have my parents here. I can't live without my brothers."

The Germans Invade

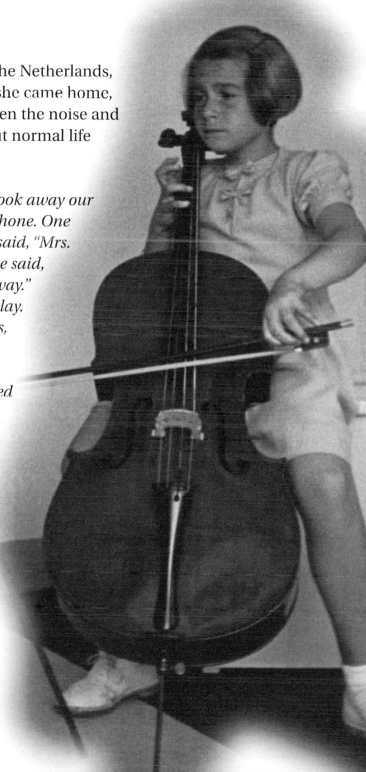

On the morning of May 10, 1940, we were awakened by noises. My father said it was military exercises. My mother said, "No, the Germans are bombing." They were throwing bombs on the military barracks not far from our house.

And that was how the war started.

Although the Germans had invaded the Netherlands, Stella went to school that day. When she came home, "there was my cello teacher. In between the noise and the bombs, we had a cello lesson." But normal life would soon disappear.

We had to wear the yellow star. They took away our car, our precious belongings, our telephone. One day, a German rang the doorbell and said, "Mrs. Splitter, may I use your telephone?" She said, "You know you took our telephones away." It was just a little game they liked to play.

When we had to hand over the cars, we went by streetcar, but we were permitted to ride on the back balcony only. And then when we weren't allowed to go by streetcar, we went by bicycle. Then they took away our bicycles and we went on foot. There was a curfew after dark, and we were allowed to go shopping only a couple of hours a day. Jews weren't allowed in public places—theaters, swimming pools, movie theaters. And I had to go to a Jewish school, with Jewish teachers and Jewish children only. We were not allowed any contact with our non-Jewish friends.

Stella playing the cello.

In the summer of 1942, they started to send out notices to report for deportation. My family's business had been taken over by the Germans. My father, his brother, and my cousins were still allowed to come to the store and work, but they were not allowed any contact with the customers or non-Jewish employees.

One day in September, none of the men came home. They had been taken away somewhere.

When that happened, Stella's mother became frantic.

My mother had a nervous breakdown that night. One fainting spell after another. My aunt lived three houses down the block but I couldn't go out because there was a curfew, and I couldn't call her because we had no telephone.

Stella took care of her mother by herself, all night.

The next morning, my cousin Mellie moved in with us. We found out later that the men were in prison in the Hague.

Deportation

On October 2, 1942, I was walking home from school with a friend when we noticed a van in front of my house. I said to my friend, "You had better go home, because if you go with me you are not going to see your parents again." Sure enough, my mother was packing two big duffel bags. We were able to give our dog to a friend, along with photos. The dog was saved, and so were the pictures.

We were taken in the van to a villa where there were lots of other people. From there we were taken to the prison. It was very dark and the walls were lined with men. Someone yelled to my mother, "Irene!" and we turned just in time to see my father being pushed against the wall. We hadn't seen him for a month.

The family was sent together to Westerbork, a Dutch transit camp. There, prisoners were guarded and kept in by barbed wire.

Children in the Westerbork transit camp. Westerbork, 1941-1944.

The family was together during the day; they separated men and women at night. We had a hot plate, and everyone had ten minutes per day to use it. My mother would cook rice and then wrap it in a blanket to finish cooking it.

Twice a week, people were selected to fill a quota the Germans set to fill cattle cars. We all were lined up, always at night, with our backpacks, waiting to see if we would be called. They told us, "We are resettling you. We want all the Jews together in one place. And then you will work for us."

In fact, most of the people removed in cattle cars were taken to Auschwitz and other camps. Very few survived.

Because of their fur-making skills, in February 1943 the Splitter family was taken to Vught, a concentration camp in the Netherlands at which furs and clothing were manufactured for Germany. Life was worse here than in Westerbork. Food was strictly rationed, and the Germans took away personal belongings bit by bit. Everyone was counted twice a day, by guards wearing uniforms and high boots.

The food was always the same: We received our bread ration at night. This was supper and breakfast. At noon we had soup. As the war wore on the bread got less and was one thin, often moldy slice. The soup got thinner. Toward the end sometimes a single leaf floated in it.

Stella and her family were in Vught for about a year. Gradually, people started to disappear from the camp. Most of those taken away were old people and mothers with children. Of the children, only Stella and three other girls remained because their fathers were important workers at the camp. Stella started working in the factory. She saw her parents there every day.

One night we had to leave our barracks. They took away all our clothing and gave us striped prison clothes. There was a lot of pushing and I was almost pushed against the barbed wire, but my mother protected me with her body so I was not hurt. The next morning when I saw my father at the factory with his head shaved and in a striped prison uniform I burst into tears. My father laughed and said that should be the worst that ever happened to him.

March 20, 1944, all the men were gathered in the camp's central square. When the women were marched back to the factory I saw my father. He waved at me from afar, and I waved at him. It was the last time I saw him.

In the factory, the women were screaming. They wanted to be with their men. My mother said, "There is no point in screaming. We all know what to do, let's continue to work." The factory lasted one month longer.

The women were moved to an electronics factory in the same camp, run by the Philips company, which had established the factory to save their Jewish employees from deportation.

Awakened in the Night

On June 2, 1944, just months before Stella's fourteenth birthday, the women in the camp were awakened in the middle of the night. The women were marched from the camp to cattle cars.

Prisoners at work in one of the Philips workshops in the Vught concentration camp. Vught, the Netherlands, 1943–1944.

We traveled four days in cattle cars to the East. We arrived someplace and heard, "Get out, get out!" There was lots of shoving. It was dark, and there were chimneys with smoke and flames coming out of them and a very strange odor in the air.

Stella did not know it, but she was seeing the chimneys of the crematoria at Auschwitz, where people who had been killed were turned into ashes. Before she learned the truth of what she had seen, she had to strip naked with all the other women, and they were shaved "under the arms and the pubic hair. It was a degrading experience."

SS officers were running around. I was very scared. I said, "Mom, I am so scared. I don't want to die." She didn't say anything. That was the

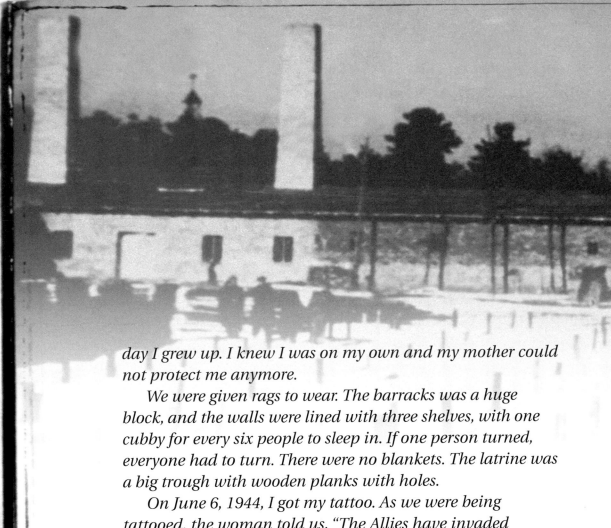

day I grew up. I knew I was on my own and my mother could not protect me anymore.

We were given rags to wear. The barracks was a huge block, and the walls were lined with three shelves, with one cubby for every six people to sleep in. If one person turned, everyone had to turn. There were no blankets. The latrine was a big trough with wooden planks with holes.

On June 6, 1944, I got my tattoo. As we were being tattooed, the woman told us, "The Allies have invaded Europe! The war will be over soon, hallelujah!" The tattoo felt like continuous little pinpricks. My number didn't take very well, and they had to do it over again.

Stella's number was 81761. It is almost as clear today as it was on the day it was made.

Separated and Reunited

A few days after their arrival, Stella and her mother were picked as slave laborers for a German factory because they knew electronics. They had a chance to leave Auschwitz! But Stella came down with a fever and was forced to go to the infectious disease barracks. Although she was fine the

next day, Dr. Mengele made her stay there for three weeks to be sure she did not come down with anything.

My mother was smuggled in to see me. She did not want to leave but since her chances of survival in Auschwitz were very slim (she was an "old woman" of thirty-six), we were able to persuade her to leave. On August 19, 1944, I celebrated my fourteenth birthday all alone in the infectious disease barracks in Auschwitz, not knowing whether either one of my parents was alive.

On November 1, 1944, someone came running to get me. "Stella , Stella, come quickly! The man is here from the factory in Germany and he wants to see you!" When I was brought to see him he said, "I bring you regards from your mother. Would you like to go to her?" What a question! Having almost lost my mother and hearing that she was alive was a gift from heaven.

When I left Auschwitz alive against all hope two weeks later and the cattle cars rode under that infamous sign "Arbeit macht frei" [work will make you free], *I made up my mind that I would do my darnedest to survive, if they let me.*

The chimneys of one of the crematoria at Auschwitz-Birkenau, Poland.

Finding Her Mother

A few days later I arrived at a camp called Sportschule. My mother was not there. I found out later that she lived in a different camp but worked at the same Telefunken electronics factory where I was taken the next day. We met in the bathroom, and the first words out of my mouth were, "Mom, how old you have become." She was thirty-six years old and looked like she was sixty. I was told she did not stop crying the whole time we were separated. When we worked the same shift, we managed to see each other a few minutes in the bathroom. If we worked different shifts, which ran from 6:00 to 6:00, we waved at each other coming and going, but we were happy to be near each other.

The war was going poorly for the Germans. We could hear the shooting at the eastern front.

After several months of working under terrible conditions and constant hunger, the prisoners were taken out of the camp in February 1945. The Soviet army was approaching, so the camp was evacuated. "We walked for four days," sleeping in fields and barns, says Stella. Their hard wooden clogs wore holes in their feet. To this day, Stella has scars on her feet from that long death march.

"Whoever straggled was not seen again," says Stella. "You had to hold on to your cup and bowl and spoon for dear life. Should you lose that, there was no replacement."

For more than two months Stella's group was moved from one labor camp to another, sometimes on foot and sometimes in open cattle cars, which were exposed to the elements. There was no protection from rain, snow , and sleet.

Once we were joined by a group of criminals. Cattle cars had a sign

The gate at Auschwitz, with the Nazi slogan "Arbeit Macht Frei," meaning "work makes you free."

saying "Eight horses or forty men."
Two hundred of us were now
crowded into a cattle car together
with murderers, rapists, and thieves.
Every day they picked out a few
people to kill to have more room
and at night they murdered them
and threw them out of the cattle
car. For four days we traveled
without food and with very little
water. We shared one red cabbage
leaf four ways. Even I started to
doubt that I would be able to
survive.

Finally, Stella's ordeal
was over. On May 1,
1945, Stella and her
mother and cousin
Mellie were
liberated in
Denmark. From there
they went to Sweden,
where they were
nursed, fed, and clothed.
In August 1945 they
returned to the
Netherlands.
   "Whenever I walked
down the street," says Stella,
"I looked for my father, hoping to find
him." In November 1945, they learned that
he had died in Flossenburg concentration
camp.

Stella, 17 years old, showing
her tattoo from Auschwitz.

chapter seven

Preserving the Memories

Many people who experienced the years of Nazi terror have had trouble talking about it later. For some, the memories are just too painful. Recently, though, more and more survivors and witnesses have decided that it is time to record their memories, so their experiences will never be forgotten or denied.

Gerda Weissmann Klein married the soldier who liberated her, Kurt Klein, in 1946. Soon thereafter, they settled in Kurt's former home in the United States. Today Gerda lives in the Southwest with her husband. They have three children and eight grandchildren. She often speaks to students about her experiences.

"I get hundreds of letters a month. Ninety percent of the letters are from teenagers. They identify, because I was fifteen years old when it all began. Many of the letters allude to the fact that they had toyed with the idea of suicide before reading *All But My Life*. They thank me for not doing it."

Teens ask her why she wanted to live. She answers, "No matter how difficult life is, you don't know what is around the corner. By no stretch of the

Gerda Weismann Klein in a recent photo.

imagination could I have thought I would make it.

Gerda returned to her hometown of Bielsko and visited Auschwitz for the first time in 1997. "It was a very good, healing experience. Difficult as the trip was, I am glad we did it because it represents a closure. I will never be able to reproach myself for not having visited the place where my parents died."

David Weiss Halivni was the only member of his immediate family to survive the Holocaust. His sister died of typhus after being liberated from Bergen-Belsen concentration camp. His grandfather, mother, and aunt were killed in Auschwitz. His father died not far from the Dachau concentration camp, bitten to death by attack dogs.

After the war, David Weiss Halivni and Tzipora Hager met in the United States and married.

David, Tzipora and two of their children.

David was ordained a rabbi and earned his doctorate. He taught, and later he founded the Institute for Traditional Judaism. Tzipora earned her doctorate and taught Holocaust history.

Today, the Halivnis have three children and one grandchild. David teaches religion at Columbia University. He published his memoir, *The Book and the Sword: A Life of Learning in the Shadow of Destruction*. David, who has never returned to Sighet, says his book is "a way of trying to explain how people persevere."

Now that he has written a book about his experience, he says, his family "would like me to go back" to Sighet, the town where he grew up. Even the Romanian government has invited him. "I have resisted," he says. "My first grandchild gives me a sense of continuity. If he asks, I may break down and go."

After the war, Stella Splitter and her mother moved to the United States. Stella got a job and was introduced to Hank Marcus, who had come to the United States at about the same time. Stella and Hank married.

When Stella talks to high school classes, she shows them a photograph of her paternal grandparents' 1934 golden wedding anniversary celebration in the Netherlands. "The whole family is together," she says. "Everyone is dressed up beautifully. And I show a picture of myself running around in the dunes."

Stella and Hank have one daughter. Stella says, "I talk about my experiences because I feel I have an obligation to educate people about the Holocaust, especially young people, so they can build a better future. I tell teens to put themselves in my shoes to better understand what happened."

Today Werner Reich, who is a retired industrial engineer, lives in the United States with his wife, Eva, who is a secretary. They have two children and one grandchild. When Werner learned that the

54

Stella running through the dunes.

local high school had a Holocaust studies program, he volunteered to talk to students about his experience. "I called up and said, 'I am living here, and if you would like, I am willing to talk.'"

Stella with her husband and daughter.

"I don't feel the world owes me anything," Werner says, "and I think maybe by talking to students I can help. I very firmly believe in God. I am not a very religious person, but I firmly believe that God created a miracle by putting us on this earth. And what we do to each other is our own doing."

As teenagers, these four found the courage to believe that they would survive the horrible conditions of Nazi concentration camps, labor camps, and death camps. After they were liberated, they realized they had lost almost everyone they loved. Somehow, they managed to build new lives, eventually starting families of their own. Today they may be happy, but they remember their teenage years as the darkest chapter of their lives. To them, it is not history. It is a recent personal experience. They hope those who know their stories will pass this knowledge on to the next generations, so that nothing like this will happen again.

Timeline

January 30, 1933	Adolf Hitler is appointed chancellor of Germany.
March 23, 1933	Dachau, the first concentration camp, is built in Germany to hold political opponents of Nazis.
April 1, 1933	Nazis proclaim a daylong boycott of Jewish-owned businesses.
July 14, 1933	Nazis outlaw all other political parties in Germany; a law is passed legalizing forced sterilization of Roma and Sinti (Gypsies), mentally and physically disabled Germans, African-Germans, and others.
January 26, 1934	Germany and Poland sign Non-Aggression Pact.
August 1, 1935	"No Jews" signs appear in Germany forbidding Jews from stores, restaurants, places of entertainment, etc.
September 15, 1935	German parliament passes the Nuremberg Laws.
March 13, 1938	Germany annexes Austria.
September 29, 1938	Munich Conference: Britain and France allow Hitler to annex part of Czechoslovakia in order to prevent war.
November 9, 1938	Kristallnacht (looting and vandalism of Jewish homes and businesses and widespread destruction of synagogues) occurs throughout Germany and Austria; 30,000 Jews are sent to Nazi concentration camps.
March 15, 1939	Germany invades all of Czechoslovakia.
August 23, 1939	Germany and Soviet Union sign Non-Aggression Pact.
September 1, 1939	Germany invades western Poland.
September 2, 1939	Great Britain and France declare war on Germany.

September 17, 1939	Soviet Union invades eastern Poland.
Spring 1940	Germany invades Denmark, Norway, the Netherlands, Luxembourg, Belgium, and France.
March 24, 1941	Germany invades North Africa.
April 6, 1941	Germany invades Yugoslavia and Greece.
June 22, 1941	Germany invades western Soviet Union.
July 31, 1941	Reinhard Heydrich appointed to carry out the "Final Solution" (extermination of all European Jews).
Summer 1941	*Einsatzgruppen* (mobile killing squads) begin to massacre Jews in western Soviet Union.
December 7, 1941	Japan bombs Pearl Harbor; United States enters World War II.
January 20, 1942	Wannsee Conference: Nazi leaders meet to design "Final Solution."
Spring and Summer 1942	Many Polish ghettos emptied; residents deported to death camps.
February 2, 1943	German troops in Stalingrad, Soviet Union, surrender; the Allies begin to win the war.
June 11, 1943	Nazis decide that all ghettos in Poland and Soviet Union are to be emptied and residents deported to death camps.
March 19, 1944	Germany occupies Hungary.
June 6, 1944	D-Day: Normandy Invasion by the Allies.
January 30, 1945	Soviet forces liberate Auschwitz concentration camp.
May 8, 1945	Germany surrenders to the Allies; war ends in Europe.

Glossary

antisemitism Hostility toward or discrimination against Jews.

Aryans According to Nazi ideology, people of Nordic or Germanic background, members of Hitler's "master race."

collaborators Non-Germans who willingly helped or supported the Nazis.

concentration camp A place where political prisoners and prisoners of war are confined.

deportation The forced removal of people from one country or area to another.

death camps Concentration camps where people considered unfit for work are racially undesirable are murdered.

death march A long march intended to exhaust concentration camp inmates, sometimes to the point of death.

detention camps Special centers set up for political prisoners and racial minorities considered undesirable.

Einsatzgruppen Mobile killing squads who killed Jews in lands occupied by the Germans.

gas chamber A room where people are killed by poison gas.

Gestapo The Nazi secret state police.

ghetto A part of a city set aside by the Nazis to contain only Jews. Ghettos were heavily guarded and lacking in food, water, heat, housing, and health care.

Holocaust The extermination of six million Jews and millions of others during World War II.

Kapo A camp inmate chosen by the Nazis to lead work teams.

Kristallnacht Meaning the "night of broken glass," November 9, 1938, was a government-sponsored attack on Jews, resulting in the destruction of Jewish-owned businesses and synagogues.

labor camp A camp where prisoners were forced into slave labor to help the German war effort.

Nazi The political party that ruled in Germany (1933–1945); full name: National Socialist German Workers' Party.

Nuremberg Laws German laws passed on September 15, 1935, that legalized antisemitism and stripped Jewish Germans of many rights.

occupation The control of an area by a foreign military force.

political prisoners People put in jail for their beliefs and opinions.

rations An allowance of food for one day.

Reich The German word for "empire." Hitler called the period of Nazi control of Germany the Third Reich, which he claimed would last for 1,000 years.

Selektion A process at concentration camps where those considered fit for work were separated from those marked for death.

transit camp (*Durchgangslager*) A camp where prisoners were held before being sent to a labor camp.

For Further Reading

Bachrach, Susan D. *Tell Them We Remember: The Story of the Holocaust.* Boston: Little, Brown & Co., 1994.

Bitton-Jackson, Livia. *I Have Lived a Thousand Years: Growing Up in the Holocaust.* New York: Simon & Schuster, 1997.

Eliach, Yaffa. *Hasidic Tales of the Holocaust.* New York: Random House, 1988.

Frank, Anne. *Diary of a Young Girl: The Definitive Edition.* New York: Doubleday, 1995.

Holliday, Laurel. *Children in the Holocaust and World War II: Their Secret Diaries.* New York: Washington Square Press, 1994.

Klein, Gerda. *All but My Life.* New York: Hill & Wang, 1995.

Rochman, Hazel, and Darlene Z. McCampbell, eds. *Bearing Witness: Stories of the Holocaust.* New York: Orchard Books Watts, 1995.

Volavkova, Hana, ed. *I Never Saw Another Butterfly: Children's Drawings and Poems from Terezin Concentration Camp.* New York: Schocken Books, 1994.

For Advanced Readers

Asscher-Pinkhof, Clara. *Star Children.* Detroit: Wayne State University Press, 1986.

Baumel, Judith Tydor. *Unfulfilled Promise: Rescue and Resettlement of Jewish Refugee Children in the United States, 1934–1945.* Juneau, Alaska: Denali Press 1990.

Dwork, Deborah. *Children with a Star.* New Haven, CT: Yale University Press, 1991.

Edelheit, Abraham J., and Herschel Edelheit. *History of the Holocaust: A Handbook and Dictionary.* Boulder, CO: Westview Press, 1994.

Gilbert, Martin. *The Holocaust: A History of the Jews of Europe During the Second World War.* New York: Henry Holt & Co., 1985.

Noakes, J., and G. Pridham. *Nazism: A History in Documents and Eyewitness Accounts, Vols. I and II.* New York: Pantheon Books, 1984.

Wiesel, Elie. *Night.* New York: Bantam Books, 1982.

Videos

Auschwitz: If You Cried, You Died
Two survivors describe their experiences at Auschwitz after a return visit there. Includes historic footage of the camp and discusses "revisionists," those who claim the Holocaust never happened. (Available from Impact America Foundation, Inc., c/o Martin J. Moore, 9100 Keystone at the Crossing, Suite 390, Indianapolis, IN 46240-2158; (317) 848-5134.)

Night and Fog
An award-winning documentary using historic footage shot inside the concentration camps as well as color footage from 1955, when the film was made. Addresses questions of responsibility and looks for echoes of Nazi actions in contemporary society. Note: Highly graphic. (Available in many libraries and video stores.)

61

Triumph of Memory

Non-Jews who survived Mauthausen, Buchenwald, and Auschwitz-Birkenau tell their stories. Looks at daily life in the camps as well as the horrors that took place in them. Includes a discussion of the fate of the Roma and Sinti in the camps. (Available from PBS Video, 1320 Braddock Place, Alexandria, VA 22314-1698; (800) 344-3377.)

Web Sites

Anti-Defamation League—Braun Holocaust Institute
http://www.adl.org/Braun/braun.htm

The Cybrary of the Holocaust
http://www.remember.org

Holocaust Education and Memorial Centre of Toronto
http://www.feduja.org

Museum of Tolerance
www.wiesenthal.com/mot/index.html

Simon Wiesenthal Center
http://www.wiesenthal.com/

United States Holocaust Memorial Museum
http://www.ushmm.org/index.html

Yad Vashem
http://www.yad-vashem.org.il

Index

About the Author

Toby Axelrod is a 1997-98 Fulbright scholar and was previously an award-winning journalist for the New York *Jewish Week*. Born in Queens, New York, she studied at Vassar College and the Columbia University School of Journalism. She is writing a book about how young Germans today are confronting their own family involvement in Nazi crimes.

About the Series Editor

Yaffa Eliach is Professor of History and Literature in the Department of Judaic Studies at Brooklyn College. She founded and directed the Center for Holocaust Studies (now part of the Museum of Jewish Heritage—A Living Memorial to the Holocaust) and designed the Tower of Life exhibit at the U.S. Holocaust Memorial Museum. Professor Eliach is the author of *Hasidic Tales of the Holocaust; We Were Children Just Like You; There Once Was a World: A Nine Century Chronicle of the Shtetl of Eishyshok;* and *The Liberators: Eyewitness Accounts of the Liberation of Concentration Camps.*

Photo Credits

Cover photo courtesy of Gerda Weissman Klein; p. 6 KZ Gedenkstatte Dachau, courtesy of the United States Holocaust Memorial Museum (USHMM) Photo Archives; pp. 8–9, 43, 51, 54, 55 courtesy of Stella Marcus; p. 10–11 © the Institute of Contemporary History and Wiener Library Limited, courtesy of USHMM Photo Archives; pp. 12–13 © American Jewish Distribution Committee, courtesy of USHMM Photo Archives; p. 14 © Abraham Preiss, courtesy of USHMM Photo Archives; p. 16 © Stadtarchiv und Landesgeschichtliche Bibliothek Bielefeld, courtesy of USHMM Photo Archives; p. 18 © Hessisches Hauptstaatsarchiv Wiesbaden, courtesy of USHMM Photo Archives; p. 19 © Robert A. Schmuhl, courtesy of USHMM Photo Archives; pp 20, 31, 36–37, 47 © Yad Vashem Photo Archives, courtesy of USHMM Photo Archives; pp. 21, 26, 53 courtesy of David Weiss Halvini; p. 23 © Mauthausen Museum Archives, courtesy of USHMM Photo Archives; p. 24 © James McEvoy, courtesy of USHMM Photo Archives; pp. 25, 35, 40–41 © National Archives, courtesy of USHMM Photo Archives; pp. 28, 52 courtesy of Gerda Weissman Klein; p. 33 YIVO Institute for Jewish Research, courtesy of USHMM Photo Archives; p. 34 courtesy of Werner Reich; p. 38 © Muzej Revolucije Narodnosti Jugoslavije, courtesy of USHMM Photo Archives; p. 39 © State Museum in Majdanek, courtesy of USHMM Photo Archives; p. 45 © Lydia Chagoll, courtesy of USHMM Photo Archives; pp. 48-49 © Main Commission for the Investigation of Nazi War Crimes in Poland, Warsaw, Poland, courtesy of USHMM Photo Archives; p. 50 © Main Commission for the Investigation of Nazi War Crimes, courtesy of USHMM Photo Archives

Series Design
Kim Sonsky

Layout
Laura Murawski